REMIND ME AGAIN

Poems and Practices for Remembering Who We Are

JOE DAVIS

REMIND ME AGAIN
Poems and Practices for Remembering Who We Are

Cover and interior image: Abstract Mid-Century Geometric Shapes Blue Gray Distorted Scratched Textured Background by Oxygen.
Copyright © Getty Images. Adapted by Kristin Miller.
Cover and interior design: Kristin Miller
Interior typesetting: Josh Eller
Editor: Dawn Rundman
Project Manager: Julie O'Brien

"Love Always" first appeared on THRED.org. "Who Is Your Everyone?" first appeared on THRED.org. "Show Up" first appeared in *Staying Awake: The Gospel for Changemakers* by Tyler Sit.

ISBN: 978-1-5064-9126-4
Manufactured in USA

27 26 25 24 23 1 2 3 4 5 6 7 8 9 10

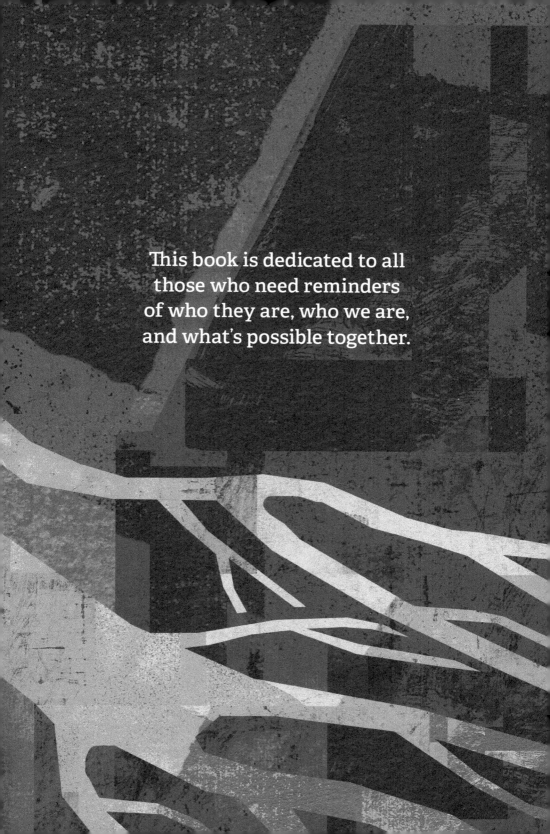

This book is dedicated to all
those who need reminders
of who they are, who we are,
and what's possible together.

To the Reader

"Charge it to my head, not to my heart." That's what I say whenever I forget something that really matters to me, but it simply slipped my mind, like someone's name or birthday.

Reminders are often helpful. I know I'm not the only one who needs them—I've seen people set multiple alarms, post endless sticky notes, and even tie strings around their finger as if to give their memory a gentle jolt of electricity.

Reminders are especially helpful when our deepest truths are forgotten, lost, or stolen.

Truths such as how to be vulnerable and courageous, how to unapologetically reclaim our bodies as good and worthy of love, and how to cultivate and sustain authentic community with one another.

As an artist, I like to write poems and songs that help us remember what matters most, what we forgot we already knew. Just like many of our elders and ancestors used poetry and song in their sacred ceremonies and rituals to stay connected to a shared sense of being, we do the same today in our communities of faith, in our school classrooms, and even in our halls of political power.

Growing up, it was playful rhymes and rhythms that helped me memorize everything from the alphabet to Easter speeches, the bones in the human body and the planets in the solar system, the names of presidents and the branches of government.

What if we deepen these already cultural and communal practices with an intention of reclaiming our full selves—our heads, hearts, spirits, and bodies—so that we re-embody otherwise disembodied truths? What if we reminded each other of the possibility of healing, wholeness, and human flourishing in such beautiful, powerful ways that the truth becomes unforgettable?

What if we "charge it" to our entire beings like a billion-voltage lightning bolt zigzagging across the blue-black midnight sky, writing our names and birthdays in cursive amongst the stars, an eternal streak of fire setting the moonlit stage ablaze with the wholly flames of who we are and all we can become?

Maybe we can respond to these questions together in the pages of this book and through the poetry of our lives. I wrote this book as if to say, "Pssst! Hey! Look over here! Have you tried this? It worked for me and my community or worked for other groups of people or worked for our ancestors. Maybe it could work for you too?"

And on the days when we need a gentle jolt of electricity to reawaken the wisdom buried within our cells and our souls; when our deepest truths have been forgotten, lost, or stolen; maybe we can turn to each other and say, "Remind me again."

Contents

My Purpose
Reminders for the World

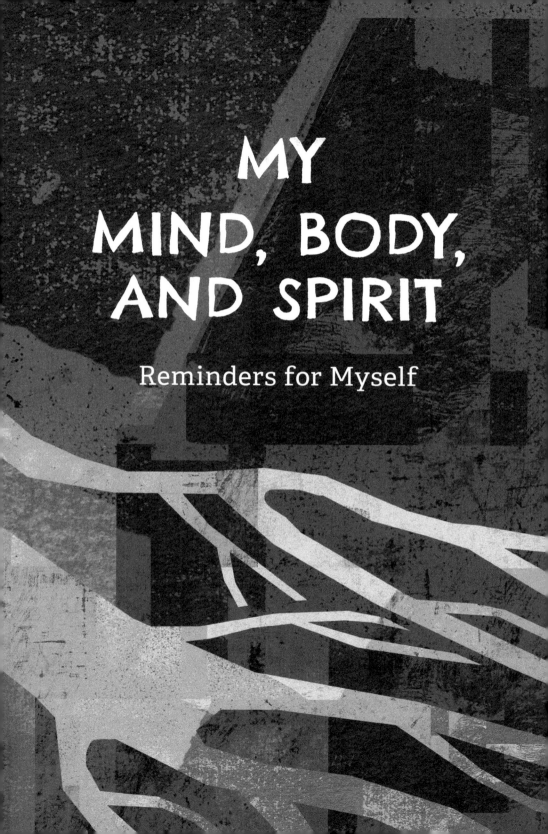

MY MIND, BODY, AND SPIRIT

Reminders for Myself

Brave Space

A reminder of where to find courage

Can there be a space for us
that feels safe enough
to be brave enough?

A space to practice loving ourselves
with vulnerable and courageous Love?

Courageous enough to be vulnerable,
vulnerable enough to be courageous—
if we can't find this place yet,
can we be brave enough to create it?

Whenever you're looking for what you've lost
and someone else is helping,
they ask, where's the last place you saw it—
but not the last place you *felt* it.

We've all been brave before,
but sometimes bravery gets misplaced,
and what it felt like in our bodies maybe needs to be retraced.

If you can't find the old path
perhaps a new one can be made—
shine your flashlight in the shade
where memory's lanes began to fade.

If fear and courage make our bodies feel exactly the same,
what happened inside of us to make the feeling change its name?

We've all heard those stories of amazing feats of bravery,
like the mom who lifts a car to save her crying baby.
Is it fear or Love that gives us superhuman feelings
to fight off packs of wolves or leap from burning buildings?

Can the stories hidden in our hearts and buried in our brains
make more space for Love to flow, like blood coursing through our veins?
Help us untangle our nerves, help us loosen our chains,
help us finally face our fears and move through our pain?

I can't tell you how to go through life and never be afraid,
but I can show you how to feel the fear and do it anyway.

When you no longer fear the feeling and begin to feel the fear
it gets smaller and smaller until it starts to disappear.

Wipe away all the dust from your mirror
so everything you face can be seen even clearer
until fear is in the rearview and hope is even nearer
and no matter where you look you see courage everywhere.

A brave space is never far away and it's never really gone —
it's the wholehearted part of you that's been there waiting all along.

Find bravery in every wall and floorboard your fingertips have ever felt,
find it in every cabinet and shelf that you have within yourself,
no more looking under cushions, in closets, or anywhere else
for it's found in the foundation upon which all of you is built.

No need for renovation or furniture rearrangement,
when it's the frame which you were made with
from the attic to the basement.

Activate places within you once thought unsafe or dangerous,
make staircases from anxiousness to excitement and motivation,
replace fear and shame with inspiration and amazement.

It's an audacious, bold, and brazen
act of risk-taking,
to rename and reclaim *yourself*
as a Brave Haven.

There can be a space for us
that feels safe enough
to be brave enough!

A space to practice loving ourselves
with vulnerable and courageous Love!

Courageous enough to be vulnerable,
vulnerable enough to be courageous—
if we haven't found this place yet,
we are brave enough to create it!

Try This Practice

What's your biggest worry, insecurity, or fear?
Feel where it shows up in your body.

What's your greatest love, joy, or hope?
Feel where it shows up in your body.

Imagine your greatest love replacing your greatest fear.
Practice feeling this in your body.

Write about a time you were afraid to do something but
you did it anyway. Describe this experience with vivid
detail, using as much sensory language as possible.
Practice feeling this in your body.

If there's one thing you're afraid of saying or doing,
practice feeling the fear and then saying or
doing it anyway.

Good & Worthy of Love

A reminder of my body's goodness

I often tried to run from my body
because it didn't feel like a safe place to be,
yet no matter how I fight or punish my body
it still chooses to stay with me.

As if it only ever wants my highest good
and was purposefully made for me.
As if love itself were stitched and knit together,
perfectly shaped for me.

I didn't organize my organs,
order my bones and hair to grow,
or explain to my valves, vessels, and veins
where blood and air should flow.

Without forcing me to believe,
no need to perform or achieve,
my body was there to care for me,
and all I did was receive.

My body pledges allegiance
to the thesis of my being,
releasing what doesn't feed me
and keeping all I need.

If I hug myself,
my body hugs back even tighter.
Every time I take a breath
my chest opens even wider.

I will stop looking for excuses not to be loved because
if this doesn't speak to an infinitely loving intent
then I don't know what does.

I am grateful for this body
for it is divine, sacred, and Godly.

I will listen to its gentle whispers
so it needn't shout so loudly:

I am good and worthy of love
I am good and worthy of love
I am good and worthy of love
I am good, I am more than enough.

Your worth is never an effort
nor earned
but adorned
when you were born.
It was inherent and apparent
from the womb when you were formed.

Perhaps this is something
you've never been told or never felt,
but I am here to help you tell yourself
until you feel it in every cell of yourself.

And although this truth
is the most beautiful truth
I could ever give you,
it is true not because I wrote it,
but because it's written within you.

You are immeasurably lovable,
every single inch of you.
You have an intricate system
dedicated to defending you.

Every softened edge and scar is hard-won.
You may not believe in miracles,
but I'm here to tell you:
you are one.

Will you stop looking for excuses
not to be loved because
if this doesn't speak of
an infinitely loving intent
then I don't know what does.

There is beauty in your body
for it is divine, sacred, and Godly.

Will you listen to its gentle whispers
so it needn't shout so loudly:

You are good and worthy of love
You are good and worthy of love
You are good and worthy of love
You are good, you are more than enough.

The body is our best friend
no matter how many times
we neglect or disrespect it.
Everything it ever did
was to keep us safe and protected,
without question.

So much time invested
trying to turn the body
into what it already is:
good and worthy of love.

Goodness moves with a boundlessness.
So much goodness surrounds us
and abounds so much
it's bound to be found deep down in us.

More than empty rhetoric or pretty aesthetic,
goodness is where we come from
and where we're always heading.

Goodness is our essence,
our natural state,
our default setting.

Our goodness will grow
and overflow
and spread
if we let it.

My body, your body, our bodies
are not meant to be discarded.

Our mother earth births bodies to be fed,
bodies to be watered.
All that we are
is to be held in love and honored.

We can stop looking for excuses not to be loved because
if this doesn't speak to an infinitely loving intent
then I don't know what does.

We can be grateful for this body
for it is divine, sacred, and Godly.

Will we listen to its gentle whispers
so it needn't shout so loudly:

We are good and worthy of love
We are good and worthy of love
We are good and worthy of love
We are good, we are more than enough.

Try This Practice

Hold one hand over your heart and one hand over your belly, soften your gaze, and deepen your breathing. Repeat these words inside your head or aloud, as many times as needed for you to believe them:

I am good and worthy of love.

If you're unable to say these words to yourself or simply need some encouragement, find someone who is willing to say them to you. Ask if they'd also like to hear these words said to them. Repeat these words together as many times as needed for each of you to believe them:

You are good and worthy of love.

It can be powerful and transformative to say these words with your community. Invite as many people as needed to repeat these words as many times as needed for all of you to believe them:

We are good and worthy of love.

Write a list of all the reasons this statement is true about yourself and about others. Revisit this list and this affirmation as often as needed.

Wounds

A reminder of healing

I cry because I can see all the wounds in your heart,
the wounds in all the places you don't feel love,
the wounds in all the places you've been hurt,
the wounds in all the places you've been abandoned and rejected,
by others
and yourself.

I cry because I would heal every one of those wounds
if I could,
but I can't.

I can only let my tears wash my own wounds
until I remember a God within me
who loves us all back to wholeness.

Try This Practice

Write a scar story, the story of how you healed one
of your biggest wounds—mental, emotional, spiritual,
or physical.

Whole Armor of God

A reminder of protection

In this war-torn world
we wear an armor of amor
with pens as swords
and metaphors
for better worlds.
We use words to fight a war
so we ain't gotta fight no more.

It's all an art.

Learning how to guard our hearts
means growing stronger hearts
that don't become hardened hearts.

And the war isn't won until we all do our part.

Try This Practice

Write, draw, or paint what it looks like for you to be in
a world of peace. Hang up what you created somewhere
inside your home.

You're Not Crazy

A reminder of who you are

You're not crazy

Maybe you're different,
maybe you're gifted,
maybe you feel downtrodden and need to be uplifted,
maybe your life has shifted and
you're tired of a life that's scripted,
you realize there's a reason why you exist and
there's nothing you're experiencing
others in history haven't persisted

You're not crazy

Maybe people called your blessing a curse,
maybe you can imagine the best instead of the worst

Maybe your dream is too big for their small mind,
maybe you don't need a co-sign
for what God already designed

Maybe you're just unorthodox
and you just think outside the box,
maybe you like to rock mismatched socks
and their awkward gawks won't stop
but don't stop
the way you like to dress, walk, or talk

Maybe you're trying to adjust to a sick society,
you don't subscribe to traditional conventional propriety,
they're too bland and you embrace variety,
they can't see the world through the same eyes you see

They're just calling you sick as if they're well,
they judge you when you fall as if they never fell

You're not crazy

Maybe your body is wanting safety
and you just started learning what safe means

Maybe there's too much on your mind,
you feel foggy and hazy,
you can't think, your thoughts are blocked
and locked in a brain freeze

Maybe life's storms are raging
and you're bracing,
although your heart is racing,
you're moving bravely
trying to keep it together
when everything else is breaking

Maybe you're overworked and
you're hurting and aching,
you've been told you're broken
but you just need a break
or vacation, you're craving
a life you're not always escaping,
or coping or caping
"Help me, save me,"
you need liberating

Maybe you're burned out, tired, exhausted, fatigued,
maybe you need a nap but you can't fall asleep

Maybe there's a lesson in the test,
maybe you can let go, take a breath and just rest

You're not crazy

Maybe you can have Jesus and a therapist
because even therapists have therapists

Maybe thoughts and prayers
can be shared with love
not just shared online
but shared with a hug

Maybe we all need someone who cares for us
and cares enough to carry us
when we can't carry us,
then the caring and carrying become
a bridge over the barriers burying us

You're not crazy

You are not defective,
you are not abandoned or rejected,
you are protected and held with affection,
maybe you only have yet to accept it

You're awesome, awe-inspiring, and amazing,
maybe some people expect you to always be the same,
but lately
you're growing and changing,
evolving and awaking,
learning from your mistakes,
bumps, and scrapes more graciously,
with less hastened speed,
more space and a pace
as slow as you may need

The only thing wrong with you
is thinking there's something wrong with you

Fight the lies, find the truth,
and ask what's right with you?

You're not crazy.

Try This Practice

Consider how and when you use the word *crazy*.

Write a list of people, places, and resources that support
you when you feel unstable or unsettled. Set the list
somewhere as a reminder when needed.

Ask others you trust if you can share your list with them
and invite them to share their list too. We create the
space for more healing and wholeness when we share
communal supports and resources.

Emotions Are Guests

A reminder to feel our emotions

Emotions are guests,
emotions are visitors—
if we sit with them,
they don't have to live with us.

Emotions are guests,
emotions are visitors—
if they are expressed,
there's gifts they can give to us.

We meet them with the same sweetness
with which they greet us.

But we get uncomfortable
when they get too comfortable
and put their feet up.

The temperature was perfect,
but they turned the heat up.

There's no more food in the fridge
for them to eat up.

They need to leave,
it's past time we speak up.

Emotions are guests,
emotions are visitors—
if we sit with them,
they don't have to live with us.

Emotions are guests,
emotions are visitors—
if they are expressed,
there's gifts they can give to us.

As we travel this path we're on,
emotions are our passengers,
and as they're passing through
they have messages they're passing us.

We are the drivers of their taxi bus,
and while it may feel as if they're taxing us,
a ride to the other side is all they ever ask of us.

Can we be more hospitable hosts for these guests in our homes
who offer us wisdom, songs, prayers, and poems?

They have messages to tell us—
we can help them help us.

They may overstay their welcome, but cannot stay forever.
Can we give them the chance to change us for the better?

Can we offer them a welcome mat, without becoming one?
Invite them for coffee or tea until the conversation's done?

Unless we give them our blessing, there's no rest yet.
Until we've fully felt them, there's no exit.

Their story's incomplete, until we've finally read it.

"This too will pass,"
but only if we let it.

Emotions are guests,
emotions are visitors—
if we sit with them,
they don't have to live with us.

Emotions are guests,
emotions are visitors—
if they are expressed,
there's gifts they can give to us.

Try This Practice

Play "Emotion Roulette." Write all the emotions you
can think of on small strips of paper and place them
in a hat, basket, or cup. Randomly pick one of the
strips of paper and try to read this poem (or others) in
the emotional tone you selected. For example, if the
emotion you select is sadness, anger, or joy, you would
read the poem with a sad, angry, or joyous tone.

Thoughts

A reminder to be mindful

Serendipity! It hit me like a symphony of thoughts!
Quickening me mentally, an epiphany of thoughts!

See, I'd be a rich man if I had a penny for my thoughts,
any of my thoughts,
I have an infinity of thoughts!
Never starving 'cuz my harvest is plenty in thoughts!

Food for thought:
if I could eat these thoughts
I would feast on thoughts,
I could survive for weeks off just a piece of these thoughts,
if I give speech to these thoughts
they grow feet and they walk,
they run, jump, skip, hop, and they don't stop!

Not even if I forgot to . . . forgot to . . . forgot to . . .
Gotcha!
I never got writer's block!
I take those blank thoughts and make great thoughts,
I build on top like building blocks until the sky scrapes the top
but I still don't stop!

I accumulate thoughts and formulate plots
and create thoughts you never thought I thought
until I cease your thoughts with ceaseless thoughts,
secrets released like eaves they drop,
know not whether I'm to teach or preach with these thoughts,
but at the very least I seek to bring peace with each thought.

Deep thoughts,
deep as seas
yet seemingly reaching peaks as I speak,
faithfully they leap
prayerfully they cleave
my soul with God—
who without
all of my thoughts
would be brought
to naught.

Try This Practice

Moving your body can help stretch your muscles and joints, increase blood flow, and help you channel your energy when your thoughts are ceaselessly racing. You can practice this whenever you need a boost! You can even try this while listening to your favorite music.

Stand up and shake your right arm as fast as you can 10 times, counting each shake as loud as you can: 1-2-3-4-5-6-7-8-9-10! Do the same with your left arm.

Now, shake your right leg as fast as you can 10 times, counting each shake as loud as you can: 1-2-3-4-5-6-7-8-9-10! Do the same with your left leg.

Repeat this with each limb, this time counting to 9. Repeat this with each limb, counting to 8. Continue to repeat this, each time shaking one less count until you get to 1. When you finally get to 1, let out a great big shout!

This can be done by yourself or in a group circle as long as you have enough space to move.

I Am Free

A reminder of where to find freedom

I am free:
to speak in my language,
to worship my God,
to heal from my pain, and
to love who I love.

Let me remind you,
you must've forgot,
I am free just as I was from the start.

Free as the drumbeat that pumps in my heart,
free as the blood, sweat, and tears in my art,
free as the sun is to dance in the dark,
to see all my people beyond prison bars.

Free is the picture I'm painting,
free is the world we're creating,
free is the image we're made in,
when they try to take it, we rise and reclaim it.

No shackle or chain can enslave us,
we remain if they try to erase us,
the hate of this world cannot break us,
we stay 'cuz our freedom is like a mosaic.

We answer the call when freedom rings,
with our freedom songs that we freely sing,
got the kingdom keys from the King of kings,
so I'm free to bring all I'm free to be—
free to breathe, free to grieve, free to be angry,
free to leave, free to scream, free to speak frankly:
I believe
I am not crazy,
I am free
the way my God made me.

Just like a tree
That once was a seed

Deep within me
Is all that I need

No one is free
Until we're all freed

When we are free
We are free indeed

Free is a lifestyle, free is a vibe,
living each day happy to be alive,
I see it shining deep in my mind,
I'm only as free as I feel inside.

I wanna reach higher than the divide,
beyond the confines of society's lines,
I wanna stretch the length of my spine,
touching the depth of what we call divine.

True liberation's why we freedom fight,
free education, we can read and write,
Freedom Schools and the Freedom Rides,
Free Breakfast Program, hold the freedom fries,
We're free 99 — we don't need a price.

We free to laugh and we free to cry,
we free to live and we free to die,
'cuz even in death
we let freedom rise.

Just like a tree
That once was a seed

Deep within me
Is all that I need

No one is free
Until we're all freed

When we are free
We are free indeed

Somewhere in mind—
it may be winter outside—
but it's summer in my mind.

Christ said inside is where we find the kingdom,
that's why my heart is a rib-caged bird singing of freedom.

I am free.

Try This Practice

Write down three things you do that help you feel joyful,
alive, and free. Schedule the time in your calendar to do
those three things every day, starting now.

Soul Stories

A reminder of the stories we hold

I am telling wholier stories about myself.
Not better or worse stories,
But whole stories,
Soul Stories.
Stories that name both the harm and the healing.
Stories that are at peace with all that I am thinking and feeling.
Stories of less doing.
Stories of more being.
Stories that give the best of all I'm receiving.

Try This Practice

Keep track of the positive and negative thoughts you
have about yourself for one day. For every negative
thought you track, try to come up with three positive
affirmations about yourself.

Reflect on how even your negative traits could be
protective or helpful if positively redirected.

Let Go

A reminder to let go

Letting go can be as easy as breathing, eating, and sleeping.

As easy as breathing,
inhaling and receiving the oxygen you're needing,
exhaling and releasing the toxins you're leaving.

As easy as eating
fruit and receiving the nutrients you're needing,
spitting out the pits and seeds you're leaving.

As easy as sleeping,
receiving the rest that you're needing,
relieved of the tension and stress that you're leaving.

When it's easier said than done, ask your soul:
What do I hold that I can't control?
If it's blocking life's flow,
how can I let go?

Try This Practice

Write down three things you want to let go of and
release them to the elements. Burn the list, let it float
away in water, or release it to blow away in the wind.

Enough

A reminder of abundance

If it's better to have it and not need it
than to need it and not have it,
then what happens if
one of us is in want?

Between you and me,
if we can be all we need,
then perhaps
who we are is enough.

Try This Practice

Write a list of everything you have and don't need.
Write a list of everything you need.

Ask a neighbor, friend, or family member to also write
the same two lists.

Look at what you've both written and see if there are
any gaps or overlaps where what's needed can be shared
by the other. This can also be practiced in community.

Love Always

A reminder of unconditional love

I love you.
I love you at your best, I love you at your worst,
I love you in a dress or sweatpants and T-shirt.

I love you when you stay in shape, I love you when you gain weight,
I love everything about you that you love and even everything you say you hate!
I love you.

I love you when you wake up, I love you without makeup,
I love you any time of day in any way because
I mean it when I say love!
I love you.

I love you from start to finish, from head to toe,
I love your every spot, wrinkle, and blemish,
every freckle and mole.
I love both your dimples and your pimples,
your mind, body, spirit, and soul.
I will love you before and after the here and now
and now I'm here to let you know,
I love you.

I love the way you laugh, you smile, you talk, you walk, you sing.
I could cut this poem in half and say I love your everything.

Because if you ever think that you're not loved
that just isn't so!
No matter what, my love for you is unconditional.

I will love you forever and a day
and today is the day I will forever say
I will love you just the same when your hair turns dusty gray,
I will love you just because I love you:
Always.

Try This Practice

Read this poem as a love letter from God.
Now read this poem as a love letter from your body.
Write your own love letter to yourself.

What do you love about yourself?
What do you find hard to love about yourself?
What are practices that would help you more fully
receive love from God, yourself, and others?

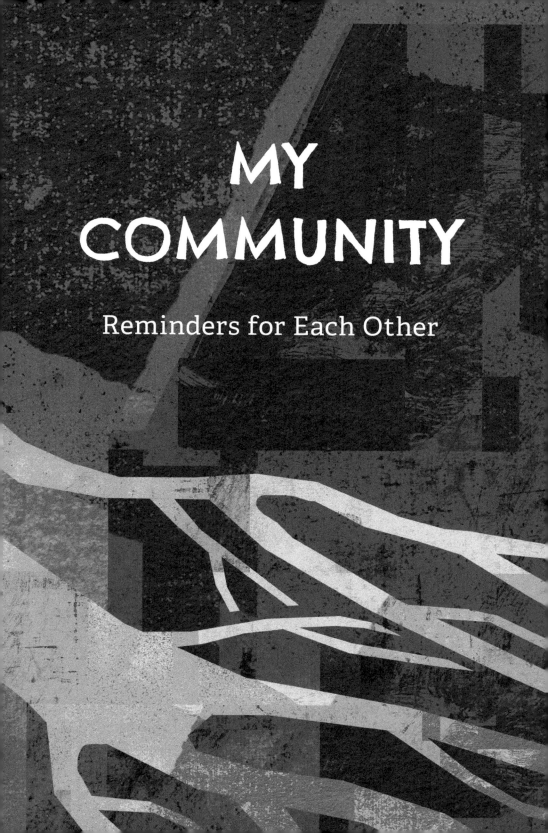

MY COMMUNITY

Reminders for Each Other

We Rise Higher Together

A reminder of what's possible together

Life is better
when we rise together.

There are possibilities
only realized together.

With your help,
I rise higher than myself.
United, we reach higher than ever.

We can climb on our own,
but we climb ever higher when we're not climbing alone.

We are not self-taught, we are community-taught.
We are not independent, we are interdependent.

I am because we are—
and everything we are is because someone loved us into existence.

The world has more than enough to share,
and all of it was meant for us.

And if what we carry is too much to bear,
then others can lift us up.

Together, more can be done,
together there's more to become.

Everyone wants their time to shine,
but the sun shines on everyone.

We shine brighter when we shine together,
we rise higher when we raise others.

Together we weather any storm
to gather a rainbow of colors.

We can't have collective healing
without the collective,
when our well-being is interconnected.

Can we rise to our highest intention?
Can we rise to love's highest expression?

Together we rise higher
than what holds us down
to common, higher, holy ground.

Together we rise higher,
like words from the page to the world stage,
like the smoke of palo santo or sage.

Together we rise higher
than the muck and the mire,
we rise even higher than crumbling empires.

Together we rise higher
like voices in the choir,
like sunflowers and sun fire.
If we fall or forget,
we'll be each other's reminder
until we're so high that our souls fly!

Together we'll rise higher and fly higher
until we rise close to the Most High.

Try This Practice

Call two or three people in your community and offer
them words of encouragement. Do any of you have
a project or task that would be better if worked on
in collaboration?

Systems

A reminder of our interconnectedness

Little systems: littler systems
Big systems: bigger systems

We are systems inside systems
above us and below us
around us and within us.

The soul is connected to the body:
the body is connected to the people:
the people are connected to the land:
the land is connected to the planet:
the planet is connected to the galaxy:
the galaxy is connected to the universe.

Whatever ism is or isn't in our system
begins or ends with us
and what every system that exists can become
depends on if we begin or end it with love.

We are intercellular and interstellar
our cells and our selves
are meant to be together.

Whether or not we believe
we interweave and we need each other.

It's the pitter-patter of patterns
a majestic map of tapestries
that tap and turn
small smatterings of star-scattered
gatherings into galaxies
like all the space and matter between
Saturn's rings.

The universe is connected to the galaxy:
the galaxy is connected to the planet:
the planet is connected to the land:
the land is connected to the people:
the people are connected to the body:
the body is connected to the soul.

Little systems: littler systems
Big systems: bigger systems

We are systems inside systems
above us and below us
around us and within us.

Try This Practice

Explore and reflect on our interdependence by filling in
the blanks with different words:

If we have _____ in our personal systems
we will have _____ in our person-to-person systems.

If we have _____ in our person-to-person systems
we will have _____ in our governing systems.

Versions of Our Selves

A reminder of our whole self

Could our best versions and worst versions
just be healed versions and hurt versions?

Higher or lower, more or less,
could be expressed versions and suppressed versions?

Do my version and your version
change with our perceptions of perfection
or whether or not we prefer them?

How many versions are abandoned, rejected, or deserted?
How many versions do we have that are accepted and nourished?

Can we know for certain how many versions we don't really know?
And how can we make sure all our versions
can flourish and be whole?

Try This Practice

Write a list of ways you show up authentically.

Write a list of ways you show up inauthentically.

Use the lists to help you become more aware and
develop practices that help you show up as your most
authentic self.

Proud and Free

A reminder of our power

We can all be proud and free.
You ain't gotta shout and sing as loud as me,
you ain't gotta bow down to me or crown me king,
we all got our own style, our own smile—
our whole self is the only thing we know how to be.

So find your own borders and boundaries,
get centered and grounded, dig down deep,
you have the same power that I found in me.
We can all be proud and free.

Try This Practice

What does your body feel like when you feel worn down
or weary? How do you hold your body when you feel
exuberant? Powerful? Joyful? Proud? When you feel free?

Notice the differences in your body when you feel these
contrasting emotions.

Future Friends

A reminder of good friends

Future friends are friends who
always keep your best intention
in mind and remind
you, when you forget,
the world can be simple, gentle, and kind

Future friends are friends who
care about your future
so when they find your wounds
their friendship starts to shape a suture

Future friends are friends
who ask you how you feel and mean it,
ask you how you're eating,
ask you, "how is your breathing?"

When you meet them
it's more than a meeting
it's two souls
with one heart beating

They're the friends who transcend time,
they're friends worth always keeping.

Try This Practice

Check in with one of your friends and create a space of
shared vulnerability.

Pace of Relationship

A reminder of life's rhythms

Life moves at the pace of relationship.
The depth of our transformation is
as deep as our grace and patience is.
It takes as long as cultivation does.

Take your time.

You can't plant the seed
and eat the fruit the same day.
You gotta cultivate the soil.

What you reap
what you think
what you speak
is a seed
that you keep
watering.

Life moves at the pace of relationship.
The depth of our transformation is
as deep as our grace and patience is.
It takes as long as cultivation does.

Take your
time.

Not just gracing the surface,
but grace at the center,
grace in the core.
When we give away grace,
we only make space for more.

What you reap
what you think
what you speak
is a tree
that you keep
watering.

Life moves at the pace of relationship.
The depth of our transformation is
as deep as our grace and patience is.
It takes as long as cultivation does.

Take
your
time.

Try This Practice

Take a walk through nature and reflect on
how life grows. Take your time. What lessons can you
learn about your relationship with yourself and others?

Good Neighbor

A reminder to be a good neighbor

If everyone is our neighbor
and the world is our neighborhood,
then what kind of behavior
does God say makes a neighbor good?

If I see a new neighbor, would I stop and stare,
make fun of their clothes, or laugh at their hair?

Or would I ask them their name
and how they like to be greeted
so I can treat them the way that they'd like to be treated?

Would I listen to their stories, their songs, their jokes?
Would I share with them my fears, my dreams, my hopes?

If we have different cultures or speak different languages,
would I want to learn more or think that they're dangerous?

And how can I make the space feel safe for them?
Are there things that need to be created or changed for them?

Are they asked to stand when they need a chair?
Do they need a ramp when we only have stairs?

If I have what they need, will I happily share?
What ways can I show that I actually care?

Being a good neighbor isn't about saving others
or behaving in ways the laws say we should,
but discovering how God's grace already makes us good,
and how God's love turns beloved neighbors into beloved neighborhoods.

Try This Practice

Meet someone new in your neighborhood, your school,
or your faith community.

Who Is Your Everyone?

A reminder about who belongs

Who is your everyone?
Is it only those in the country you were born in?
Or migrant workers whose customs and cultures may seem foreign?
Does it only mean those in your church Sunday morning?
Or the nonreligious, or Jews, or Muslims, or Mormons?
With whom does your "everyone" begin or end?
Is it only those with your zip code, your language, your skin?

Can your vision extend beyond "us versus them"
toward a bridge of love where true justice bends?
Where all our walls crumble and fall
between "those people" who make us feel most uncomfortable?
Different and distant, they seem so unlovable—
but we will come to discover: God loves them too!
No more or less, but just as much as you!

This is the truth we often may forget:
that of a transformational relationship
when we celebrate everyone's human sacredness.

For we are them and they are us, all created in God's image.

Who is your everyone?

Try This Practice

Draw a circle within a circle. In the innermost circle, write
the names of people who are loved, accepted, and affirmed
by society. In the outer circle, write the names of people
who are unloved, rejected, and abandoned by society.

What are actions you can take to help erase the line
that separates those on the inside from those on the
outside? Invite others to join you in these actions.

Call Out / Call In

A reminder of how to hold each other

We put our right foot in
and take our left foot out.
We put our left foot in
and take our right foot out.

Call out / call in. Call in / call out.
Healing relationships is what it's all about.
But how can we return to a right relationship
if a part of us is always left out?

Hurt people hurt people,
heal people heal people:

We've all been a part of this wheel before.

Yet we still forget and we still ignore,
it feels less like a dance and more like a war.

Pointing fingers, placing blame,
hurling shame like a grenade.

What roles have yet to be named?
What mistakes have yet to be claimed?

We know this dance can't stay the same,
but do we still believe in change?

Not a dance of revenge and resentment,
offering an offense for an offense,
taller fences of intolerance,
it's all unresolved and endless.

Unless we admit that we've all been complicit.
We are not faultless, sinless, guiltless,
we all have a part within this,
and are called to confession and repentance.

Only those who own the brokenness
can then begin to mend it.

How far beyond ourselves are our arms extended
to close the gap and go the distance?

Call out / call in. Call in / call out.
Healing relationships is what it's all about.
But how can we return to a right relationship
if a part of us is always left out?

Are we listening to the call to join a new dance?

One with enough nuance / for our two arms
to hold both compassion / and correction
to hold both accountability / and connection?

To let go of hard punishment or harsh judgment /
and hold closer the call for a heart of abundance.

To call out those struggling /
and in need of another chance
to get back in touch with /
their missing belovedness.

To call out the person / without discarding them,
to call out the harm / without further harming them.

To call out of disconnection and displacement /
to call into deeper authentic relationship
To call out of disparity and scarcity /
to call into community and solidarity
To call out of a hopeless view of humanity /
to call in the possibility of all we can be.

Can we pull each other from under / the weight of our woundedness?
Can we move through the pain / without it consuming us?

If we don't choose forgiveness / does forgiveness choose us?
How long will it take / to learn this new dance?

Can we acknowledge the hurt / and commit to reparative work?

To call out and call in our highest intent
until our intent is in alignment
and we find the rhythm
for which you and I were meant:
Call out / call in. Call in / call out.
Healing relationships is what it's all about.
We can we return to a right relationship
when we're all in / and no one's left out.
Even when we step on toes, stumble, and fall,
will we get back up and answer the call?

Try This Practice

Write about a time when you were wronged or when
you wronged someone and were able to work toward
repair. Reflect on the lessons you can learn and carry
forward from calling out and calling in.

Bully-Free Zone

A reminder of the power of friendship

Bullying begins when
the bullying within
becomes bullying without
and that bullying begets bullying
everyone else

But what if everyone else
could be there to help
heal the bully
and let them fully
be the best of their selves?

Try This Practice

Think about a time you bullied yourself or others.
Bullying can mean being harshly judgmental, unfairly
critical, unkind, or ungracious. Ask yourself why this
happened. Then explore a more compassionate response.

big kids

A reminder to honor the kid in all of us

big kids, big kids,
no longer little kids,
no matter how big we get,
we still got an inner kid.

we can't return to the bliss
of ignorance and innocence,
but can we tend with tenderness
to the inner child who lives in us?

as grown as we think we are,
can we still see the world
with curiosity and awe?

like if we fall
off a swing or seesaw,
can we crawl back to joy
even with our knees raw?

what if joy was bigger than your body
and grew bigger than you?

is the big you just a little you
who grew from within you?

can you find other big kids who
can grow young with you?
who can be serious enough
to still have fun with you?

making sand castles and mud pies,
chasing ice cream trucks and fireflies,
with grass stains and bright eyes
can we still be surprised

at how a child can get knocked down
but can somehow still rise?

big kids, big kids,
no longer little kids,
no matter how big we get,
we still got an inner kid.

Try This Practice

Give yourself permission to be silly, playful, and have fun.
Go do something that would make the kid in you proud!

Elder Songs

A reminder to honor our elders

This one goes out to all the elders,
the foreparents we all cherish,
the truest treasures of every village,
the greatest and grandest among us,
forever serving
bellyful bowls of soul songs

crisscross applesauce,
I so long to sit at their feet
to slowly sip and drink deeply,
to sway and rock with their heartbeat
while in wooden chairs
as they drop gems and jewels
more precious than gold in silver hairs

fingers tracing the wrinkles on their faces,
reading between the smile lines of their eyes,
pages of old-school sayings and funny phrases,
leg-slapping laughing with living libraries
of stories so scrumptious
they stick to your gut

they hum humility into us
from every verse to chorus refrain,
teaching us how to remain through
both bitter and sweet days,
a bridge to endless gifts
pressed in the palm of my hand
like Sunday candy

we are their gathered-round children,
the miracle and medicine of their wisdom
can guide and heal us
if only we have the ears to listen

we honor the elders,
those who are still here with us,
or those who have gone on into the great beyond,
by saying their names, telling their stories, and singing their songs.

Try This Practice

Reach out to an elder in your life. Spend some quality
time with them and show them how much you care.
Maybe you can tell a story or sing a song together.

Ancestral Echoes

A reminder to honor our ancestors

Answering the ancestral echoes of our origin,
we wonder how near or far the call is:
From the stars or in the dust?
Foreign or indigenous?

The Creator's provisions
hidden within the rhythms
pulsating against our skin,
against our skin,
against our skin.
The Creator's provisions
hidden within the rhythms
pulsating against our skin.

I walk in the strength of 4,000 ancestors
who loved me into existence,
who loved me through their persistence,
who love me wherever I stand—
they're standing with me
and nothing can stand against us.

I claim both the horror and glory
of all those who came before me.

And I carry forward the best of them.
They survived so I could be alive,
and now I am a living testament
through which they resurrect again
from the tomb of my chest
as it lifts, every breath is evidence
that their spirit still takes residence,
pregnant with precedence,
a legacy resonant with every step,
every step,
every step.
A legacy resonant with every step.

Through hopes and
hardships
they crawled and marched across
oceans
unbroken to return home again,
whole again
within my soul holding them
as close as skin
like an anointed book of sacred songs
and holy hymns,
psalms in the palms
of my open hands,
open hands,
open hands.
Psalms in the palms of my open hands.

Answering the ancestral echoes of our origin,
we wonder how near or far the call is:
From the stars or in the dust?
Foreign or indigenous?

The Creator's provisions
hidden within the rhythms
pulsating against our skin,
against our skin,
against our skin.
The Creator's provisions
hidden within the rhythms
pulsating against our skin.

Their history of victories
lets us know we are so much more
than any tragedies or traumas.

The greatest tragedy is actually
those who deny and dishonor us.
Under every trauma
is the healing wisdom and resilience
it took to move beyond it.

Regardless of what they call us,
we are not an oppressed people,
we are a liberation people.

We grow to become what we practice most,
we are not the sum of the worst that ever happened to us,
we are the culmination of the mysterious, the magic, and the miraculous.

Answering the ancestral echoes of our origin,
we wonder how near or far the call is:
From the stars or in the dust?
Foreign or indigenous?

The Creator's provisions
hidden within the rhythms
pulsating against our skin,
against our skin,
against our skin.
The Creator's provisions
hidden within the rhythms
pulsating against our skin.

Try This Practice

Write a letter, poem, or song to honor one
of your ancestors, naming the gifts you've inherited
from them. As an embodied act of memorializing, read
or sing what you've written out loud.

Humanity (Ubuntu)

A reminder of who we are

If I could have any superpower in the world it would be
to make everyone everywhere feel true empathy;
not just some simple, sentimental, emotional coexistence,
but a deep, heart-wrenching, soul-clinching conviction
to feel as another feels,
see as another sees,
breathe not only the same air,
but with the same lungs another breathes:
life,
a life lived with
instead of against,
and then we would understand what it means to understand,
learning to let mercy have the upper hand.

Not splintered in self-centeredness
but our family's reunion re-membering and re-mending
into an interdependency so intimately linked
we begin to befriend even our enemies,
as the strong defend the weak,
bowing to empower the gentle and the meek,
Muslim, Jew, and Christian, poor and rich, soldiers and politicians,
fathers and children would all change positions, not of opposition

but
walking in opposite skin, likewise eyes exchanging visions,
until we bear the single burden of sharing the same difference,
then we would witness what only an altered heart can see—
the death of division and birth of empathy.

The only superhuman ability I really need
is the instilling of universal vulnerability,
for there's no truer form of virtue and nobility
than to repay harm with help or return hate with humility,
to trade revenge and retaliation
with forgiveness and relation.
If we see no space for love, then it's our choice to make one.
We cannot save the masses if we do not first save one,
and until that day comes
we will sing the same song:

One hope,
One blood,
Many nations,
Many tongues,
Many languages of one love,
Many tribes, many races, but one family:
Humanity.

Try This Practice

Ubuntu is a South African concept, ethic, and way of
life that means "I am because we are" or "A person is
a person through other people." It was popularized by
Archbishop Desmond Tutu and Reverend Dr. Martin
Luther King Jr. as a beautiful practice to help us realize
how deeply interconnected we are as human beings.

Can you recall a time when someone different from you
was able to show up for you in a real way? Have you
ever done the same for someone different from you?

How can this kind of action be authentic, mutually
beneficial, and reciprocal, and not exploitative,
tokenizing, or performative?

MY PURPOSE

Reminders for the World

Advent of Hope

A reminder of patience

The conception of hope
isn't always immediate
but is immaculate.

I've seen hope and I know
Hope breathes and has skin.

Hope hasn't left yet,
Hope is coming back for us.

Hope happened then
and Hope will happen again.

But before any adventure
there is always an advent.

And so we wait:
for patience is a process,
and so we wait:
for patience is a practice,
and so we wait:
for we were in the past, tense,
but now we know to let go
as the present has gifts.

Hope clears a pathway
with each sacred passage.

We stretch it and stack it
step after step,
breath after breath,
"Bone of my bone,
flesh of my flesh."

It's only between
each moment of rest
we finally see
Faith made manifest.

And so we wait:
for patience is a process,
and so we wait:
for patience is a practice,
and so we wait:
for we were in the past, tense,
but now we know to let go
as the present has gifts.

Hope is not an accident,
Hope is handcrafted,
Hope is beholding the miraculous—
a body re-membered in a moment of baptism.

Hope is homecoming,
returning back to self
and feeling that Hope
grow in everyone else.

Hope whispers in the silence,
gently waiting and asking if
we can find God's presence
echoing in the absence.

Try This Practice

Humming can be a self-soothing sound that lowers
stress, calms the heart rate, and grounds and centers
our nervous system, especially during times of waiting.
When reading the poem, hum each time you reach
the italicized refrain. You can hold the hums as long or
as short as you'd like. Pay attention to how the sound
vibrates throughout your mouth, head, throat, and chest.

Begin making low, deep humming sounds with your
mouth. Slowly begin crouching down to the ground—
the lower and deeper the sounds, the lower and deeper
you can crouch your body.

Now begin making a higher-pitched humming sound.
The higher your hum becomes, the higher you can
move upward, even if you're stretching as high as you
can toward the sky. Go up and down the major scale,
keeping your mouth closed.

Begin making a slow humming sound while moving,
matching your pace with the pace of your humming.
Play around with the speed of your humming and
moving, going faster and slower, faster and slower.
You can even go back and forth between crouching
and stretching. If you're feeling creative, add whistling
and singing.

Finding Your Why

A reminder of our purpose

What's your North Star?
What's your soul mission?
What choices lead to your flourishing?

What wakes you up in the morning
or keeps you awake at night?

What makes your heart sing
or gives you strength to fight?

What are the wrongs in the world you want to make right?
What makes you feel joyous and fills you with light?

Finding your Why
is asking the next most faithful question,
making the path as you step in that direction.

Finding your Why
is the puzzle piece your soul fits,
no denying something inside
is enlivened and you know it.

Finding your Why
is discovery and discernment,
you may not always find it
but you'll keep on searching
because the journey in itself
unearths a deeper purpose:

Affirming you're worth it,
sometimes with words,
sometimes it's wordless,
won't always feel certain,
won't always look perfect,
but can stir up courage
and self-assuredness.

Finding our why is like exploring love.
Finding our why is like a well
that can replenish and nourish us.

When our Why is clear,
so is the way before us
and benevolent forces
join to support us.

Try This Practice

Consider these questions when discerning an
important choice:

Does it increase my aliveness?
Does it increase the aliveness of those around me?

How does it feel in my body?
How does it feel in my spirit?

What would happen to me or those I love if I didn't
do this work?

The Waiting Game

A reminder to take action

Have you ever been waiting on someone who was waiting on you
but they didn't know you were waiting on them
so you were both waiting on each other
not knowing
that you were both waiting on each other?

What if that *someone*
was actually
your *life*?

Try This Practice

What's that one conversation, task, or project you've
been waiting on? Just go do it!

Show Up

A reminder to show up as your full self

We were each called to this place,
this time and this season.

You may not yet know the rhyme or the reason,
you may not feel, think, or believe in
the same things I believe in,
but we've each been asked to show up.

Show up from wherever you are from,
you can come here to be free,
bring your full self:
both your head and your heart, your hands and your feet,
and anything and everything infinitely beyond any duality:
your sexuality, gender, race, age, and ability—
we all have the ability to be.

Without you I am incomplete,
without you there is no we,
I need you not just to survive, but to thrive,
to come fully awake and alive
with potential and possibility.

Join me at The Table for it is wide
and there is lots of food to eat.

So show up
and be fed
and feed others,
satiating a different kind of hunger,
fueling the fire in our bellies.

You matter no matter where you've been or what you've done,
all will be well when we're all welcome
to laugh, cry, dance, write, breathe, and bleed into the margins,
following the call into the farthest reaches of who we are,
whether we run, walk, crawl,
even if we fall,
we fall in love,
but just show up.

Show up to answer a call to justice,
to transform both the soul and the bodily world the soul inhabits.

Show up with all your awkwardness and bad habits,
show up with your doubts and questions,
knowing here you can ask them,
show up with your wounds and scars,
we all have baggage,
but know this is a place where, together, we can unpack it.

This is no coincidence, you are not here by accident,
you are here to share the stories of your sacred passage,
you are the only you there ever has been,
you are not the Magician, you are the Magic.

So show up to this place here,
where there is no grace period
only grace, period.

Bring your fears and insecurities,
let us marvel in the mystery,
let us listen each other to life with deep, holy listening.

Can you hear it? Can you hear it?
The sound of the genuine within you,
the Spirit stirring near you,
but if you don't show up,
how can anyone hear you?

Show up
even if you don't know for certain,
you may have the truth and healing for which the world is searching.

In this grand universe, we are but small workers
with a big purpose,
because of our hearts widening the circle,
hearts that are broken,
hearts that are open,
so a little light can shine through
a little hope for the hopeless.

Wherever you go
simply know
the Spirit of this place goes with you, so go.

Readied with sleeves rolled up,
always growing, never fully grown up,

Ready with all your heart,
mind, body, and soul,
simply to show up.

Try This Practice

Search online to find a video of me performing
this poem. Listen to the words again.
What do you notice about the poem?

Don't Show Up

A reminder for when "showing up" just ain't it

If this could've just as easily
been a text or an email instead of a meeting,
don't show up.

If you filling their quota is all that they're needing,
don't show up.

If you would go but then wish that you would've stayed,
don't show up.

If you're being overworked or underpaid,
don't show up.

If you'd rather literally be doing anything anywhere else,
don't show up.

If you being there would jeopardize your mental health,
don't show up.

If you don't need a survey, a graph, or a chart
to know that this place can't properly care for your heart,
don't show up.

If they say they want you now
but didn't want you from the start,
don't show up.

If bringing your full self
would somehow make you wrong,
don't show up.

If you need to keep you heart soft
but your boundaries strong,
don't show up.

If it will make you question your safety or your sanity,
don't show up.

If they'll honor their comfort more than your humanity,
don't show up.

If they don't enthusiastically support
your choice to be sober,
don't show up.

If you're being offered a seat at a table
your ancestors would've flipped over,
don't show up.

If they want to jump to healing and repair
before they confess and repent,
don't show up.

If they assume they know what's best for you
and don't practice consent,
don't show up.

If there are parts of yourself you have to deny or hide,
if it doesn't make you feel more healed, whole, and alive,
if the world needs you well and you need to rest,
if you need to let your "no" make room for your "yes,"
don't show up.

Because "no" is your choice.
Because "no" is your commitment.
"No" needs no explanation because "no" is a complete sentence.
No need for punctuation.
No need for exclamation.
No need for an apology
when you're allowed to just say it.

You can reclaim your time
and reclaim your space—
and for all you've given away
you can receive more grace.

Because sometimes the best way to *really* show love
to others *and* yourself is when you *don't* show up.

Try This Practice

Is there a commitment you can cancel because
it is **weighing on you? Don't show up!**

Wholly Water

A reminder of where we come from

More than swimming lessons
are taught by the water.
More than sinking or floating,
doggy paddling or back stroking,
we are soaking in an inner knowing,
ripples and waves,
ebbing and flowing.

Cycles and phases:
solid, liquid, and gas,
always connecting and changing its form,
always resurrecting, renewed and reborn.

Never any more or any lesser,
never any worse or any better,
water stays wet and can't get any wetter.

May we also remember to stay in our essence
no matter what happens around us.
Once we know we are the ocean
the waves can no longer drown us.

When we cry,
when we sweat,
we bleed medicine,
a healing blend of water and salt,
recalling the waters of our womb,
waters of the sea and sky,
where the earth meets the firmament,
where life was birthed
and will return again.

We are one body of water
circling around and swirling within.

Try This Practice

Pour yourself a glass of water. Reflect on how water is
life, and express gratitude before drinking, perhaps
with more intentionality than usual.

Love Like Fire

A reminder about healing justice

This is for all those whose love for healing and justice doesn't wax cold
but grows stronger with the breath of our ancestors.
When I say love,
I mean a love like fire.

Some run from it,
some run to it.

How you just now feelin' that fire
when we already done been through it?

Some burn flags, crosses, and Bibles.
This fire burns inside us to fight for survival.

Some shed blood from gunfire of rivaling rifles.
This fire comes 'cuz it's time to ignite a revival.

This that Holy Ghost fire!
Set it off—make ya whole soul light up!
Inspire the sick and tired to get up and fight for they life
till there ain't no mo' sick and tired.

Not violent or coerced,
but a gentle guiding force
like a vibrant torch
giving light and warmth.

Not a riot, but uprising
from love as a deep, abiding source.

C'mon hit me with the chorus:

I wish somebody's soul would catch on fire,
catch on fire, catch on fire,
I wish somebody's soul would catch on fire,
burning till we're healed and whole.

Some things we need to retrieve
and some things we need to leave.

Let it burn.

If this is an upheaval
then some things we need to upheave.

Let it burn.

If we're limited or freed by our beliefs
then what do we even believe?

And what are the necessary means
to let our people breathe?

Burn our grief and rage into the flames of liberation,
burn your guilt and shame into the flames of reparations.

Each flame is an anguish
which can't be tamed and contained in language.
It burns away chains and cages
until all that remains is
all that we're made of,
and all that we're made of is love.

What needs to die and why won't we let it?
What needs new life to be resurrected?
And must death always be a prerequisite?
This is the process of perfection and we're not perfected yet.

It may burn but it's not meant to burn us,
it may hurt but it's not meant to hurt us,
but free us from our burdens,
refine, purify, and purge us,
until the fruit-bearing root buried beneath the surface re-emerges.

We won't be consumed,
we'll blossom and bloom,
we'll rise like a butterfly who's shed its cocoon.

We will rise
like God gave Noah the rainbow sign.
No more water—
it's fire this time.

I wish somebody's soul would catch on fire,
catch on fire, catch on fire,
I wish somebody's soul would catch on fire,
burning till we're healed and whole.

This fire is cleansing.
This fire is healing.
Don't try to conceal what this fire's revealing.

It's the breath of our ancestors that we breathe.
As we shout our demands in the street,
their blood flows through our hands and our feet
no longer waiting for their chance to be free.

Try This Practice

The difference between burning up and burning down
is intention.

Light a candle and say a prayer for lives lost unjustly.
Find words or images from books, newspapers, or
magazines that symbolize violence and injustice—or
write or draw them yourself—and burn them with the
flame from the same candle. Allow this flame to burn as
long as possible.

Breath of God

A reminder of spirit

We believe in the breath of God,
a rhythm in our chest,
a movement from heaven to heart
and outward to everyone else.

We believe in the breath of God,
that hovers over the face of the deep,
that moves until every captive is freed,
that gives until no one is left in need.

We believe in the breath of God,
we will use this breath to speak
for those who can't breathe,
to weep with those who weep,
to grieve with those who grieve.

We will use this breath to practice what we preach,
to become God's hands and feet
in the church and in the street.

We believe in the breath of God,
creating justice, revealing love
beyond buildings, but the resilience God builds in us.

To confess, repent, and repair
not in guilt, blame, or shame
but through courage and compassion
until our humanity is reclaimed.

We believe in the breath of God,
to help our unbelief,
that we might give our every breath,
until we all can breathe.

Try This Practice

Breathe in through your nose for 3 to 5 seconds and imagine the wings of your lungs expanding and your belly filling up like a balloon. Breathe out for 8 to 10 seconds and imagine your belly button touching your spine.

Deep, slow breathing can help soothe and calm your heart rate when you're feeling nervous or stressed and can improve mental, physical, and spiritual well-being.

You can practice deep breathing whenever your body is overactive and needs to relax. Place your hands over the left side of your chest and pay attention to the rhythm of your heartbeat vibrating against your palms. As you take three deep breaths, notice how your chest moves with each inhale and exhale.
Repeat these words with each breath:
I breathe in God's love for me.
I breathe out God's love for the world.

Do this again, this time placing your hands over your stomach and paying attention to how your belly moves with each inhale and exhale.
Repeat these words with each breath:
I breathe in God's love for me.
I breathe out God's love for the world.

Do this one more time, this time stretching your arms upward on the inhale and downward on the exhale.
Repeat these words with each breath:
I breathe in God's love for me.
I breathe out God's love for the world.

God Is . . .

A reminder of the divine

God . . .
Is . . .
With . . .
In . . .
Us.

The source
of all light and life and love,
the lifeblood of
the universe: the one word
to one chapter to one verse to birth heaven and earth,
before and after, the first breath to stretch across
a bridge from a dark abyss to impart a kiss
pressed against the empty lips of existence:

God . . .
Is . . .
With . . .
In . . .
Us.

Beyond the lips,
beyond the script,
beyond description
of words and worlds.

An awestruck wonder
underneath the involuntary movement
of heart or blood or lungs or
every secret change whispered down the infinite ear of mystery:

God . . .
Is . . .
With . . .
In . . .
Us.

Try This Practice

Write down what you believe about God and what you
don't believe about God.

Write down what you believe about yourself and what
you don't believe about yourself.

Write down what you believe about your community
and what you don't believe about your community.

Reflect on the relationship between these three and
note any differences or similarities.

(K)New Jesus

A reminder of embodying heaven on earth

Leaning against the stained-glass window of the church library,
half lifted up and half lying on the ground,
we found a painting of white Jesus
now colored brown.

None of us knew who drew this beautiful "anachronism,"
this ingeniously subversive "historical revision"—
but Jesus' "tan" was scribbled in crayon,
so we assumed it was one of the children.

Was it their intention to draw our attention
to centuries of tension between race and religion?

Or was it simple and innocent, no hint of dissension,
just a child's description of the face they envisioned?

Maybe it was meant as divine intervention
for all of us addicted and obsessed with images,
those grumbling and grimacing at any semblance
of a Jesus outside their limited lenses.

Many insisted this was inconsistent with scripture,
others revered it as a mirror with the clearest picture
of bronze feet and wooly hair,
but it wasn't long until it wouldn't be there
and our image of God was removed out of fear.

As if cleansed with bleach, sterile and sleek,
a new revised version was there the next week.
It perplexes me why we'd try to make a martyred Savior sexy
and yet he often offended religious sensibilities.
If he came back he'd say,
"Stop it, you're killing me!"

But surely we'd crucify him again and again,
accusing him of the worst of our sins.
With drunks and criminals as friends,
he'd immediately be arrested and condemned.

His felonies would be many,
but the news would list them:
he shouldn't have resisted,
he had wine in his system,
he broke the law, he was too radical—
it wouldn't matter,
his life wouldn't matter at all.

His crucifixion was a state-sanctioned public execution.
But if we knew him today, what would we do to him?
Incarcerate him, electrocute him, or shoot him?
If he was in a police lineup, would we choose him?

Will the real Jesus please stand up?
If Jesus is the answer, is that why he has his hands up?

But Jesus was known more for how he asked questions.
They wanted to stone him because his queries were threatening
and showed all those listening their own reflections.

Does Jesus look like me?
Does Jesus look like you?
Is his likeness in our hue or what we say and do?

Why did he live? Why did he die? Why did he say "Go and do likewise"?
He had a way of truth and light that he invited us to try.
He gave his life to empower us to rise.

His birth, life, and death
were to resurrect
what love looks like
in the flesh.

We can author eloquent sermons and speeches,
but if it's not embodying love
then it don't look like Jesus.
We can educate scholars at the highest level of genius,
but if it's not embodying love
then it don't look like Jesus.
We can masterfully craft history's greatest opus or thesis,
but if it's not embodying love
then it don't look like Jesus.

Do people see *him* when they see *us*?
Do we treat *them* how he treats *us*?
What will he say on the day he greets us:

"Depart from me, you workers of iniquity,"
or "It's not too late to re-embody and re-member me"?

Can I embody the image God intends for me?
Can we become the Body we were meant to be?

Can we hold healing in our hands and carry gospel with our feet
and can we see the face of Jesus in everyone we meet?
Can we sit at the table with littlest, last, and least
until it's wide enough for us to all pass the peace?
Can we share the last of our supper, turn every famine into feast
until there are no starving children and every family can eat?

That's the image of Jesus that I want us to see.
That's the image of Jesus that I want us to be.

I am awaiting a second coming,
Spirit imbued.
I need my Jesus raw, real, honest, and true,
more than a famous first-century Jew,
moving beyond a steeple, a pulpit, a pew,
a healing for the people dying and destitute.

With the mask off the mascot, out-the-tomb Jesus,
with scars and bruises, a black-and-blue Jesus,
not the hot-and-cool, fashionable new Jesus,
but what it looks like to live like we actually *knew* Jesus.

Try This Practice

Commit one day to looking for Jesus in unexpected
people and places.

Many Ways to Pray

A reminder of diversity

Some have folded hands
Some have open hands

Some bow down low to the ground
Some walk around or stand

Some read words from sacred ancient pages
Some speak tongues of many languages

Some have tearstained faces
Some clench their jaws and shake their fists

Some hum harmonies or sing with joyful shouts
Some are quiet, sit in silence, and don't even open their mouths

Some close their eyes
Some behold the skies

Some cross their legs or do a dance
Some light candles or water plants

Some are self-reflective
Some are introspective

Some reveal confessions
Some are filled with questions

Some need contemplation
Some need meditation

Some need a quiet place to stay in like a spiritual staycation
Some feel they levitate to heaven's gates without changing physical location

Some pray in the shower, in their car, at an altar, or on a mat
Some wait until they get somewhere or pray right where they're at

Whatever they say
wherever, whenever they pray
there's more than one way
and it's okay
however they pray

Try This Practice

Try a new prayer practice that you're unfamiliar with.
See if it resonates or connects.

Faith Language

A reminder of how big God is

How do you sing the name of God in other languages and tongues?

Creator, Source, Spirit, Most High, Holy One?
With thousands of verses and thousands of years we've only just begun.

To sing the song of the divine is undone,
our human hearts have only but a hum.
We can't assume we knew it all,
the infinitely unknowable.

How can we behold a being that holds our soul?

A child in the womb knows their mother only in part,
only in the utter dark,
and yet the child is the one closest to their mother's heart,
hearing it beat after beat
from the inside and underneath,
deep crying out to deep,
a melody in sync.

Not a prison,
but a prism
that glistens when the light hits it.

When singing with the Great Mystery,
is there a right or wrong way to respond?
Or can we delight in the light
shining through the diamond of our songs?

Try This Practice

Read a text or sing a song about God that is outside of your
faith tradition. Reflect on the similarities and differences.

Transform

A reminder of transformation

Content warning: This piece mentions racial and gender violence, but it's meant to open a pathway toward healing and transformation.

Energy cannot be created or destroyed, only transferred or transformed.

The energy of violence is trapped in so many of our bodies.

This is the same energy that was in the bodies that crucified a man on a cross and that same energy blew through the bodies that watched.

And yet we forget.

This is the same energy that was in the bodies that burned women at the stake and that same energy blew through the bodies that watched.

And yet we forget.

This is the same energy that was in the bodies that lynched men on trees and that same energy blew through the bodies that watched.

And yet we forget.

This is the same energy that was in the body that knelt on a man's neck on the street and that same energy blew through the bodies that watched.

And yet we forget.

That same energy is trapped in so many of our bodies.

And we'll stay stuck in this cycle of violence—enacting it
and watching it—until we transform the energy.

Energy cannot be created or destroyed, only transferred or transformed.
This is the history we repeat today.

And yet I remember there is another more abundant, more generative,
more life-giving and life-affirming energy.

This energy lives in our bodies too.

This is the same energy in the bodies of a community crying together,
healing together, eating together.

May we remember.

This is the same energy in the bodies of those feeding schoolchildren
through the free breakfast program.

May we remember.

This is the same energy in the bodies of those sharing lunch counters,
bread baskets, soup kitchens, family cookouts, gardens.

May we remember.

This is the same energy in the body of a man eating dinner
with his best friends.

May we remember.

Do this in remembrance:
we re-member
a body
dismembered by violence
becoming whole again.

May this be the time we resurrect a radical remembrance of
the wholly family.

May we remember.
And may we be transformed.

Try This Practice

Whether through film, books, or songs, start a
collection of stories about transformation. Reflect on the
times you've experienced transformation in your life.

Prophetic Imagination

A reminder of how to change the world

Think about it, write it down, and say it out loud,
Feel it in your body when you're moving around,
Sing alone and together, you and a crowd,
Let your voices rise like a beautiful cloud.

What sensations do you want to feel on your skin and in your hair?
What aromas and scents do you want to fill the air?
What bursts of flavors do you most want to taste?
What sounds and vibrations do you want to resonate?
What textures and colors can you find to paint
The sacred and profane, the sinner and the saint?

We all got a spark, we just came to fan the flame,
We all got a part in whatever we can make.

Life's a sculpture, put your hands up in the clay,
Dip your toes in the water, let the dance take shape.

Try This Practice

Create a vision board with images of people and places
you want to pray for or hold in your heart. What are
your most courageous and compassionate hopes for the
future of the world—and what are actions you can take
to bring those hopes to life?

BE: The Church

A reminder of the world we are co-creating

The church is dying
but the church will live again
when we pass on life-giving culture and traditions.

Not death-dealing weapons
but our best healing instruments.

You can't be unchurched or overchurched
when YOU'RE the church.
God's work is our work.

Don't have to say goodbye to high church or low church
if we hold space for highs and lows of all those who soul search
and don't turn them away when they say their soul hurts.

When the body is a temple
everything is a ritual.

Re-embody and re-member
the truth you already know.

Each moment we breathe we become *ecclesia*
when we meet wherever the Spirit is leading us.
If the Bible is a library of letters and metaphors and not a book of facts,
what would it look like if we loved and lived like our life was a book of acts?

Instead we took an axe to hack chapters, burned green pastures,
and made pastors into slave masters.

Our first love is calling us back to practice.
Can we remove barriers to Hope so we all have access?

Plan A was always plan BE:
to *be* the change
to *be* the church
to *be* God's hands and feet
to *be* God's justice standing in the street

They can kill a revolutionary, but can't kill a revolution.
They can't stop our movement if we always keep it moving.

When we remember how we, the church,
are called to be the church,
we'll clothe and feed the people
who need the people of the church–
the kingdom can be within us and heaven can be on earth.

The church is living and breathing.
The church is birthing and bursting
with new life and new meaning.
The church is rising and thriving
and will flourish beyond four walls
when we're building beyond the building
a world that works for all.

Try This Practice

This is a "body blessing" or "body prayer" that one of
my friends and I lead in our racial justice communities
of practice.

Find a partner who you can pray with and who
will pray with you. You can repeat these words and
movements, but you're also invited to come up with
your own words and movements.

Place your hands over their head and pray:
May your mind be the mind of Christ.

Place your hands over their eyes and pray:
May your eyes see the face of Christ in all those you encounter.

Place your hands over their ears and pray:
May your ears hear the cries of God's children.

Place your hands over their mouth and pray:
May your mouth speak hope and truth with power and love.

Place your hands over their hands and pray:
May your hands bring healing justice to all you touch.

Place your hands over their feet and pray:
May your feet carry the good news wherever you go.

Place your hands on their shoulders,
symbolizing their heart and pray:
May your heart be filled with the love of God.

Go in peace and serve the Lord.
Thanks be to God.

Now go and be the Church!

Acknowledgements

I offer deep, heartfelt gratitude to Mother Henderson, S'sense Adams, Kirk "Bro Sun" Washington Jr., J. Otis Powell?, Andrew Thomas, Mel Reeves, Dr. Joi Lewis, Resmaa Menakem, Marlon Hall, adrienne maree brown, and Prentis Hemphill.

Your practice, work, and play serve as gentle yet powerful reminders in my life.

You remind me again and again what's possible together.